Original title:
Life's Purpose: Still Trying to Figure It Out

Copyright © 2025 Creative Arts Management OÜ
All rights reserved.

Author: Elias Marchant
ISBN HARDBACK: 978-1-80566-192-4
ISBN PAPERBACK: 978-1-80566-487-1

The Art of Questioning

Why is the sky so blue today?
Is it happier than I am,
Or just a mood it loves to play?
Clouds are my only fan.

Should I wear socks with crocs or not?
Fashion rules are quite absurd,
I think I'd rather be a robot,
Content in silence, no word.

Is there a manual for this mess?
Or do we wing it all the time?
An instruction book wouldn't impress,
If my life is just a rhyme.

What's the secret to success, I wonder?
Do I need a lucky charm?
Maybe just some endless thunder,
To shake me off my calm.

Pages Yet to Be Written

My story's blank, like a page,
With scribbles all around,
Is this a teensy bit of rage,
Or am I joyfully unbound?

Should I write of dragons or cheese?
Do wizards like to swim?
If my tale is sure to please,
Why does my plot feel so slim?

I'll add a twist with a cat, maybe,
A rescue mission for a shoe,
The ending could be quite hazy,
A surprise party for a zoo.

Every scribble is a chance,
To dance between the lines,
But why does my pen prefer to prance,
On coffee stains and vines?

Between the Lines of Existence

In the margins of my day,
I write down thoughts quite wild,
Like why socks never seem to stay,
Or why I feel like a child.

I ponder if my cat can read,
She stares at me, just blinks,
Does she know my every deed?
Or does she plan to sneak drinks?

Is there a comfy chair for thought?
One that never creaks or groans,
With cushions for each battle fought,
While I mull over my tones.

I wonder if the ants make plans,
Or is it just small talk?
Do they hold tiny hands,
On their ambitious long walk?

Driftwood in a Restless Sea

Riding waves like a lost sock,
Floating, twirling, never still,
Do I follow the tide's mock?
Or steer my own wild thrill?

A sailor's life, do I dare claim?
Or am I just driftwood afloat?
Seeking fortune, or just fame?
My boat's really just a coat.

The ocean speaks in cryptic rhyme,
With whispers of salty jest,
I'm anchored in this wavy mime,
As seabirds plan their quest.

Should I build a raft or just float?
Perhaps a party for the fish,
With a cake made of seaweed, a boat,
That grants every silly wish.

Beneath an Everchanging Sky

Beneath the sky so vast and wide,
I ponder where my dreams reside.
Should I chase a fish or climb a tree,
or just sit back and sip some tea?

Clouds float by, they change their form,
like my thoughts in every storm.
Should I paint the sky or build a fence?
Why does decision make no sense?

Letting the Wind Decide

The wind whispers secrets in my ear,
as I stand here, unsure and near.
It nudges me left, then pushes right,
as I dance in circles, lost in flight.

With every breeze, I toss a coin,
Will I find purpose or simply join?
Maybe I'll follow a stray dog's bark,
or find my way home in the dark?

Reflections of a Wayward Soul

In the mirror, I see a blur,
a face that's smiling, that's quite a stir.
Each day I wake, I check my chart,
hoping some wisdom will fill my heart.

With coffee cups stacked to the sky,
I ponder questions, oh me, oh my!
Like socks that vanish in the wash,
what do I seek? All I hear is 'posh'!

In the Quiet of Unknowing

In quiet moments, I sit and stare,
at life's game of truth or dare.
Should I juggle oranges or play the flute,
or scribble nonsense in a suit?

The answers hide like socks under beds,
while I wear doubts like fluffy threads.
Maybe I'll nap, it's an art, you see,
and let the universe unravel me!

Paradox of the Everyday

I wake up to coffee, it spills on my shoe,
The toast is on fire, but hey, that's my cue.
I make plans for greatness, but trip on my cat,
The universe chuckles, "Ain't that where it's at?"

I try to be focused, my mind's on a spree,
Dancing with dishes, oh where could they be?
I argue with socks, they've vanished in pairs,
In each little chaos, are life's hidden flares.

Tides of Uncertainty and Resolve

I ponder the future, it's blurry and stark,
Like choosing a movie, without any spark.
Should I chase the big dreams or nap on the floor?
These choices are maddening, who could ask for more?

I plan out my dinner, a gourmet delight,
End up with cereal, but hey, that's alright.
The microwave smiles, as I feign gourmet,
Each bite is a treasure, in a silly buffet.

The Whispering Heart of Existence

The heart wants to wander, but legs want to rest,
In pajamas I think, is this truly my quest?
I shop for the meaning in aisles of the store,
Found a coupon for joy, guess I need one more!

I scribble my dreams on the back of a napkin,
At least it looks fancy, though plans may be slackin'.
The laughter of friends fuels what I can't find,
We're all just confused, but we're not so blind.

Through the Cracks of Certainty

I thought I had answers, they slipped through my hands,
Like grains in the hourglass, playful in strands.
I built up a castle from dreams made of sand,
But the tide danced in, as I tried to withstand.

I wrote down my goals on a giant balloon,
Then sent them to orbit, or maybe just noon.
With each little mishap, I gather my wits,
With laughter and chaos, I embrace all the bits.

The Canvas of Hope and Doubt

I paint with colors bright and bold,
Yet splash on doubts that never get old.
The brush slips here, a stroke goes there,
Are these my hopes or just despair?

A canvas full of mismatched dreams,
Where laughter bursts at the seams.
I step back, squint one eye tight,
Is that a masterpiece or just a fight?

Each splatter tells a story, I guess,
Of coffee breaks and life's big mess.
The palette's rich but oh so strange,
My heart's a canvas, forever in change.

With every layer I try to see,
If paint can show what's really me.
So here's to trials, with a grin and shout,
I'll paint my whims, my hopes, no doubt.

A Dance with Destiny

I twirl with fate, a clumsy dance,
Trip on dreams, not quite a chance.
With two left feet, I spin around,
In this ball of awkward, joy is found.

My partner - a twist of misplaced glee,
Laughing as I step on my own knee.
We glide on floors, oh what a sight,
As destiny rolls her eyes in delight.

The music plays a wobbly tune,
I laugh and twirl under the moon.
Holding hope like a slightly cracked vase,
In this odd waltz, I find my grace.

So if you see me tripping past,
Join the dance, it's quite a blast.
We'll fumble, fall, with spirits free,
In this silly jig called trying to be.

The Elusive Horizon

I chase the sun, it runs away,
Like thoughts of bills on a sunny day.
Each step I take, it gleams and glows,
Yet somehow seems just out of throes.

With every dawn, I sprint anew,
But clouds come in, painting skies blue.
I ponder hard, should I slow down,
Or keep on sprinting in my clown gown?

The horizon laughs, a teasing mirage,
It hides behind mountains, a bold barrage.
I wave and shout, but it giggles too,
Ah, the chase is silly, but what else to do?

If I catch it, will I just sigh,
Or run in circles as years fly by?
So here I go, with a wink and grin,
Chasing sunbeams, let the fun begin!

In the Labyrinth of Thought

Wander through mazes, oh what a thrill,
With walls of doubt and a clap of will.
Every corner hides a riddle or a joke,
How many paths before I choke?

A sign says 'left,' I go to the right,
Stumbling on secrets, what a delight!
With each twist, logic gives way,
To whims and giggles, hip-hip hooray!

I stumble upon a four-leaf clover,
Now who knew thoughts could be more over?
Finding meaning in nonsense galore,
In this quirky maze, I want more!

So here I roam, with a cheeky grin,
In this labyrinth where I begin.
What's the exit? Who cares? Let's shout,
In the puzzle of thoughts, I dance about!

Searching for Signposts in the Dark

I wander through the night sky,
Hoping for a neon sign.
But all I see are shooting stars,
Giggling at my clumsy climb.

I ask a tree for wisdom,
It nods and drops a leaf.
I'm still confused and dizzy,
Nature's 'help' is quite a thief.

With every twist and turn I take,
I trip on my own two feet.
The universe is chuckling,
While I just can't find my beat.

So I dance through midnight's chaos,
Embracing every silly fall.
Even when I lose my way,
I laugh, because that's the call.

Footprints in the Sand of Time

I step into the soft, warm grains,
Wondering where they might lead.
But the tide rolls in like a prankster,
Washing away my every deed.

Each print gets swallowed whole,
Like my plans for the week ahead.
Do I follow the shore's guidance?
Or just sit here and eat bread?

I chase a seagull for answers,
But it just steals my fry.
With every snack I offer,
It laughs, as if to say 'Why?'

So I giggle at my journey,
Though my map's turned inside out.
If it's a chase for meaning,
At least I'm on a route.

The Symphony of Uncertainty

I tried to conduct my own life,
Waving my arms up high.
But it sounds more like a kazoo,
And everyone just passes by.

The flute plays off-key notes,
While the drums are out of sync.
Somewhere in this mad orchestra,
I wonder if I need a drink.

A tuba blares a funny tune,
As I step on stage with flair.
The spotlight's just my neighbor's lamp,
I'm feeling quite the heir.

But in this comical cacophony,
I shimmy and I sway.
Perhaps this noise is music,
Just a weird, wild cabaret.

In the Garden of Could-Have-Been

I tended my dreams like daisies,
But they wilted by noon.
The weeds of doubt grew thicker,
As I hummed a funky tune.

I watered my hopes with coffee,
Sun-tanned under faux-glow.
But the roses here are plastic,
What was I expecting? Who knows?

I pruned with reckless abandon,
Yet, they laughed and all fell down.
Afternoons grew slow and silly,
In my plant-filled, joyful frown.

So I dance among the faux blooms,
Choosing joy in every spin.
In this garden of mistakes,
I'm finally free to grin.

Searching for Soliloquies in Solitude

In the quiet corners, I often ponder,
What's the point of this big blunder?
Should I chase the cheese or the moon?
Maybe I'll figure it out by noon.

The cats seem wise, just lounging about,
They nap all day, without a doubt.
Should I join them, avoid the grind?
Or keep on searching, losing my mind?

Conversations with coffee, my daily chat,
It gives me courage, though it's just a flat.
Should I talk to the plants, seek advice?
They haven't moved, could they be nice?

In the end, it's a circus ring,
With juggling acts and a bee that sings.
Maybe the purpose is to just float,
While wearing mismatched socks, like a boat.

Rhythms of the Untold

I dance with my slippers, quite a sight,
To find the meaning feels just right.
Each step a question, each spin a clue,
But I just step on my cat, oh boo!

The clock ticks loudly, like a drum,
"Tick-tock, when will you become?"
I throw confetti at the ceiling fan,
Because that's a plan, right? Yes, I can!

The sandwich I made is a masterpiece,
Yet talks back, saying, "You'll never cease!"
Should I eat it or let it be?
It seems to want a degree, you see.

With rhythms of laughter that echo and play,
Who knew confusion could brighten the day?
I twirl in circles, a whimsical scout,
With every misstep, I figure it out.

The Melodies of Uncertainty

Singing in the shower, it's quite a tune,
Searching for wisdom from the moon.
The shampoo bottle gives me advice,
"Stop overthinking, just roll the dice!"

Roaming through thoughts like a lost balloon,
Every idea floats away too soon.
Should I write it down or let it fly?
That's the question, oh my, oh my!

Chasing the squirrels, they seem to know,
While I'm stuck here, moving too slow.
They gather acorns, plotting a feast,
While I just snack on leftovers at least.

But the melodies linger like a sweet refrain,
Each laugh and mishap, some joy, some pain.
In this dance of chaos, I find my song,
And maybe that's where I truly belong.

Starlit Paths and Hidden Doors

In the dark, I hear a clatter,
Is it fate or simply chatter?
Raccoons dance, I lose my phone,
Searching for a path unknown.

Glimmers shine on winding trails,
Map in hand, but where are my mails?
I step on ants, they march in rows,
All this for a snack, I suppose.

An Odyssey of the Unwritten

With a pen that seems to fly,
I scribble notes, ask the sky,
My coffee's cold, my thoughts are hot,
The universe must find my spot.

Page to page, I take a leap,
Sleeping cats in dreams so deep,
Yet here I sit, amidst the fuss,
Lost in plans named 'daring bus.'

The Seeker's Heartbeat

I check my pulse, it says 'Whoa!'
Dodging tasks that make me glow,
Is that a purpose or a game?
Last I checked, it felt the same.

Chasing dreams while eating fries,
Spilt ketchup on my hopes and lies,
But what's a path if not a giggle?
At least my heart still does a wiggle.

Navigating Through the Chaos

Maps are great but mine's a joke,
Who knew lost was part of folk?
I trip on visions, flip the page,
Dance with doubts, ignite the stage.

Juggling thoughts like fruit on stands,
Life's a circus, unplanned bands,
But in this mess, I find my ground,
With laughter loud, I'll turn around.

Barefoot on the Road of Belonging

With no shoes on, I simply roam,
Chasing dreams that smell like foam.
Potholes beckon, saying 'hi',
Yet here I am—no reason why.

Friends around me, quite the crowd,
Each with quirks, at least allowed.
We're lost in laughter, then we trip,
Together on this wild road trip.

Maps are crinkled, coffee's cold,
I swear we just found treasure—gold!
But it's really just a bumpy ride,
Still, who needs shoes when you're this wide?

So dance on asphalt, skip through grass,
With every step, let the worries pass.
We're barefoot bound, no grand design,
In this crazy adventure, we're just fine.

Seeds of Aspiration

Planting seeds in soil so strange,
Watering thoughts, watch them arrange.
A sprout of hope, but it grows slow,
Where's the handbook? I don't know!

Sunshine's bright, or is it rain?
My inner garden feels so vain.
Weeds of doubt push through the ground,
But I giggle, make silly sounds.

Pollinators buzzing, oh so sweet,
Mixing wisdom with some deceit.
I'll dance with butterflies, it's a must,
While awaiting growth, with endless trust.

So here I stand, with muck on my toes,
In this patch of dreams, anything goes.
Let's throw confetti, let laughter ring,
In this messy garden, who knows what spring?

The Symphony of Uncharted Notes

Playing tunes on off-key days,
With instruments made of play and praise.
I hit the wrong note, my cat gives a stare,
Yet still I strum with flamboyant flair.

Music notes float like butterflies,
Dancing wildly under painted skies.
An orchestra of chaos, don't you see?
My heart's conductor, wild and free.

Horns and drums clash in happy cheer,
Neighbor's frowning may I disappear?
But joyful rhythms can't be confined,
To my offbeat song, I am aligned.

So let's compose, no sheet in sight,
Harmony birthed from sheer delight.
With every blunder makes laughter bloom,
In this symphony, there's plenty of room.

Unraveled Threads of Intention

Knots too tight in this ball of string,
Tug and pull, look—what chaos I bring!
Tangled dreams in a woven mess,
But hey, it's cozy, I must confess.

Stitching moments with giddy flair,
In a patchwork world, I'm unaware.
Colors clash, patterns amiss,
Yet somehow in this, there's simple bliss.

The needle pokes, makes me frown,
But "oops!" I giggle, can't wear a crown.
With threads undone, I'll weave anew,
Creating a quilt, just for my crew.

So here's to the messiness up ahead,
With unwound yarn, and paint for thread.
In this tapestry, we'll find our way,
With love and laughter leading the fray.

Maps of the Unseen

I bought a map with no details,
It promised fun, but lost all sales.
Trekking paths that lead to nowhere,
Caution: you might find an empty chair.

The X marks treasure where I stood,
But all I found was an old shoe good.
I asked a squirrel for directions clear,
He just scurried off, didn't want to hear.

I speculate on routes less taken,
Found a pizza joint, my plan's not shaken.
I'm charting courses with guffaws and grins,
In the grand quest of where laughter begins.

So here I wander, map in hand,
Plotting mischief across this land.
The scenery's wild, the plot's a mess,
At least I've got pizza, nonetheless!

Threads of Hope in a Shattered Weave

My tapestry hangs, in colors bright,
Yet one strand's gone, oh what a sight.
I stitched and pulled, it just unraveled,
Now it resembles a song that's traveled.

Each thread I find is quite absurd,
A hopeful pink, a terrible bird.
I tie them back with a laugh so loud,
This masterpiece might attract a crowd.

So here I sit with needle and thread,
Creating chaos from what's been shed.
It may not match but oh the cheer,
Every little stitch brings joy near.

Hope gleams bright in this messy art,
In tangled yarn, I've made a start.
With each goofy knot, I feel so free,
What fun it is to just be me!

The Mystery of Being Untethered

In a world where the anchors don't hold tight,
I float and drift, what a hilarious flight!
I asked a balloon where I should go,
It just bobbed and said, "I don't know!"

Untethered dreams fly like confetti,
Land on rooftops, how very petty.
I chase the clouds, they giggle and tease,
My feet on the ground feel the whimsy breeze.

Up in the air with ideas bizarre,
I ponder purpose like a shining star.
But every bright notion gets caught in the wind,
And off they go, who needs them pinned?

So I'll sail with joy, no ties in sight,
Embracing the chaos, it feels just right.
With laughter as fuel, I'm flying free,
In the circus of life, it's all a spree!

Beneath a Veil of Questions

Under the veil of inquiry wide,
I peek to find answers, they tend to hide.
Is it pizza, or travel, or maybe a cat?
Each question just dances, imagine that!

I ask the wise sage, a goldfish in glass,
He wiggles and bubbles, through thoughts I pass.
"Why am I here?" I earnestly prattle,
He blinks and replies, "A fun little rattle!"

I ponder a tiger, then an odd sock,
Yet their advice makes me feel like a rock.
"Be wild!" they say, "but don't go too far,
Adopt an old friend, or just be bizarre!"

Questions keep swirling, like leaves in a breeze,
They tickle my mind, my thoughts never cease.
So wrapped in confusion, I dance and I sway,
Finding joy in the puzzle, come what may!

Trying to Compose Myself

I brewed some tea and thought a while,
But found my socks misplaced in style.
A symphony of chaos on my floor,
I wonder what I'm really looking for.

With lists and charts I plan my day,
A dance with purpose, come what may.
I grab a snack and lose the scheme,
Oh look, a cat! Now that's my dream.

What's this? A thought that takes a spin,
Is finding meaning where I begin?
Every wrong turn's a new delight,
Maybe life's a game, just play it right!

So here I sit in disarray,
As wisdom winks and laughs away.
I'll sum it up in words so fine,
Perhaps the answer's in the wine.

Ciphers of Tomorrow's Longing

I penned a note to future me,
"To solve the riddle, drink some tea."
But looking back with froggy eyes,
I'm sure my thoughts are grand in size.

A treasure map that leads to snacks,
Where clues are hidden in the cracks.
A silent quiz I make each day,
But all I find are books of gray.

I joke with clocks, they tick and tock,
Their answers seem to clack and mock.
With every step a zigzag dance,
Their mystery holds me in a trance.

But in this tangle, laughter grows,
For every maze is just a pose.
Solving riddles with a grin,
Maybe the secret starts within!

The Welcome Mat of Possibility

I rolled out mats for chance and whim,
And greeted puzzles, bright and dim.
With coffee cups and quirky hats,
I beckoned in a flock of cats.

Each feline pranced with aplomb,
They say they know the world's a calm.
I served them fish and joined their chat,
As they explained where wisdom's at.

The doormat's worn, the paint is chipped,
But every guest is well equipped.
A gathering of unforeseen glee,
I see them smiling back at me.

So when you knock, just take a seat,
The welcome mat's a grand old treat.
Embrace the mix of all things odd,
For seeking joy is quite the prod!

Journeys in Third Person

They packed their bags for a trip they'd take,
All paths looked tough—was that a lake?
They fumbled maps and forgot their names,
Yet laughed aloud at silly games.

With scribbled notes and quirky quotes,
They plotted routes on paper boats.
Oh, how the compass danced askew,
Did they just take a wrong turn — two?

As moments passed in slapstick haste,
They downed a snack, no time to waste.
Through twist and turns, they called it fate,
Perhaps the lost meant something great?

In shining laughter, they found their way,
Revealing sunny paths each day.
For every step holds joy's delight,
And wandering is what feels just right!

The Puzzle of Becoming

In a world of mismatched socks,
I search for my own box.
Jigsaw pieces everywhere,
Yet none seem to pair.

I tried to fit in a round hole,
Forgetting I'm a quirky soul.
Maybe I'm a rainbow in a grout,
Or a fish that just can't swim out.

Each day's a riddle in disguise,
With folks who wear glasses and ties.
I stumble and fumble, feeling astray,
But I laugh as I wander my way.

So pass me a puzzle, let's see what sticks,
I'll make it work, though it may take tricks.
With a smile I'll sort through this colorful mess,
Each twist and turn's an amusing guess.

Echoes of What Could Be

I hear whispers in the night,
Of dreams that just might take flight.
The echo of plans that go boom,
And turn into an unexpected room.

I pictured a castle with gold-plated stairs,
Only to find a house full of bears.
They greet me with honey and a dance,
As I ponder my next grand chance.

Each choice feels like a game of charades,
With clues in winks and bizarre parades.
In a world where Mondays play tricks,
I chase after visions like wild circus flicks.

Are those paths real, or just shades of me?
Like soap bubbles drifting carefree.
I'll keep chasing the fleeting glow,
Laughing where the dreams will flow.

Navigating the Fog of Ambition

In a fog that's thick like morning's brew,
I squint at the goals I thought I knew.
With a map written in invisible ink,
I trip on ambition, but still, I think.

Is that a lighthouse or a disco ball?
Maybe it's both, not one at all.
I'll dance through the haze, not fearing the fall,
Embracing the whimsy, having a ball.

Each tick-tock from the clock has its beat,
Yet I'm stuck in a rhythm that's rather sweet.
With dreams like balloons caught in the fray,
I'll float through the fog, come what may.

So hand me a compass with glitter inside,
And we'll find our way with a silly stride.
In this fog of ambitions, I'll giggle and stray,
And maybe, just maybe, we'll figure the way.

Wondering Where the Path Lies

They say the road's paved with good intentions,
But mine's covered in lost dimensions.
I walk in circles, chasing my tail,
With a map drawn by a fabled snail.

Directions from a toaster didn't help,
Nor did the wisdom from a sleeping kelp.
I asked a tree but it just swayed,
Is this wisdom, or just a charade?

The fork in the road looks like a pizza slice,
One side for fun and the other, not nice.
With a giggle, I ponder the silly options,
Will I find joy or just more concoctions?

Perhaps I'll build a bridge out of jokes,
And sail it across with dreamer blokes.
At the end of this wander, I might find the prize,
A world bursting with laughter and infinite skies.

Between the Lines of the Unknown

I woke up today, what's the plan?
Coffee first or a quick run, man?
The socks I wear, mismatched and loud,
Is this the style? I say I'm proud.

Plans on paper, all jumbled and tossed,
Should I be serious? Or be the boss?
Running in circles, a dance with fate,
Hoping I'll figure it all out, but wait…

Why is the cat staring at me?
With that look, it knows all my history.
A trip to the fridge, is it a quest?
Or just a snack, I can't really guess.

So here I am, on this great ride,
With questions galore, I laugh, I abide.
In this absurdity, I find my cheer,
Maybe it's all clear, or maybe it's unclear.

Scribbles in the Margin

I scribbled a note, tucked under the bed,
But where's the reminder? It's all in my head.
Coffee on the table, or is it tea?
Who will I be today? Let's just wait and see.

The dog thinks I'm crazy, does a floaty dance,
Is he my muse? Or just taking a chance?
With all these doodles on the pages I jot,
I'm half an artist, or just a bit fraught.

A plan to the moon, or just to the store?
What is the budget for fun? I want more!
I trip on my thoughts, like shoes untied,
Life's a sketch with crayons, let's take a ride.

At the end of the day, did I win or lose?
I can't draw conclusions, just silly hues.
With laughter and whimsy, I scribble away,
Each doodled moment makes me want to play.

Chasing Shadows of Destiny

A shadow over there, is it a sign?
Or just my reflection, feeling benign?
I chase it around, what a comical sight,
But hey, why not? It gives me delight!

Destiny's playing hide and seek, oh so sly,
Hiding behind trees, or just in the sky.
I twist and I turn, looking all around,
Maybe it's laughing, or should I be crowned?

I sat for a moment, a ponderous pose,
What if my path is just full of prose?
A potholed road? Or an express lane?
Either way, you're seeing me, chasing again!

So here's to the shadows, the light-hearted path,
To finding the fun in this silly math.
I'm still on the quest, what's next in the plot?
A life full of giggles, that's what I've got!

The Art of Meandering

Today's agenda, it reads like a maze,
Left turn, right turn, in this curious haze.
Nothing is sacred, all plans on the floor,
Why rush the journey? There's so much in store.

Picnic or potty? I can't quite say,
Got lost in my thoughts—oh, where was I, hey?
Each twist and each turn, a laugh to be found,
Like dancing on air, I'm blissfully unbound.

So here goes the clock, tick-tock, what fun,
Should I sit on the bench, or run just to run?
With snacks in my pocket, a grin on my face,
I find my own rhythm, it's a jocular race.

At day's end I ponder, what's the grand scheme?
Did I uncover a gem or just chase a dream?
With the art of meandering, I truly believe,
Every silly detour is a chance to achieve.

The Compass of the Soul

When I woke up today with a plan,
My coffee just laughed, said, "C'mon, man!"
I scribbled my goals on a taco shell,
Then tripped on my dreams, oh, what the hell?

The GPS said, "Turn right at the moon,"
But my car's stuck on an old cartoon.
I'll just chase the cats; they seem to know,
Where the best sunbeams and pizza go.

Hues of an Undefined Journey

I painted my path in colors so bright,
With crayons I found in the fridge last night.
Each shade reveals a new twist or turn,
Yet the brush just giggles—what will I learn?

A rainbow of thoughts dances in my head,
The squirrels suggest I stay in bed.
But up I rise, with pancake dreams,
Chasing my purpose in whipped cream streams.

Navigating the Unknown

With a map made of jelly, I chart my course,
Each step is a giggle, a tumble, a horse.
I yell at the stars, "What am I doing?"
But they wink back—guess they're just looming.

A compass from Burger King spins in my hand,
Pointing me to where I do not understand.
But wherever I wander, I'll bring some fries,
And laugh as I trip over each surprise.

Whispers of the Unfinished Path

The path I wander is full of quirks,
With squirrels who chat in their fancy smirks.
I search for signs that shout, "You're the best!"
But all I find is a bird with a nest.

I bought a fortune cookie for wisdom's call,
Its message? "Don't worry, just have a ball."
So I dance with my doubts, I laugh and I spin,
In this funny little journey, it's good to begin!

In Search of a North Star

I set my compass, but it spins,
As I chase my tail, where to begin?
The map is blank, like my coffee cup,
But I'm still rolling, can't give up.

A squirrel distracts, oh look at that!
Maybe the stars just talk to a cat.
I'll trade my hopes for a slice of pie,
And search for answers in a cherry sky.

The GPS says, "You're NOT there yet!"
I laugh and dance, no reason to fret.
Maybe north is just where I sit,
With snacks and joy, I'll call it a hit!

So here I ponder, with chips in hand,
Mapping dreams while building a sand.
The north star giggles, it twinkles bright,
And I toast to this absurd delight!

The Tides of Ambition

Riding waves of the next big craze,
I take a plunge, caught in the haze.
Ambition pulls me, a slippery fish,
But can't find the hook to reel in my wish.

Each tide that rolls brings fresh surprise,
My goals float by, on nacho pies.
It's a buffet of dreams, I just can't choose,
Add more toppings, what do I lose?

With a surfboard made of whimsical thoughts,
I paddle through currents, all twisted knots.
An octopus waves, says, "Follow my lead!"
But can he explain what I'm meant to heed?

So I ride on through this ocean wild,
Like a clueless yet optimistic child.
With laughter bubbling like sea foam bright,
Maybe I'll figure it out by night!

Threads of Uncertainty

I'm knitting a sweater, but it's full of holes,
Each stitch I make, my ambition rolls.
The yarn keeps tangling, what a big mess,
Is this fashion? Or is it distress?

My thoughts spiral like spaghetti strands,
Is this art? Or did I drop my plans?
I tie a knot, but it just unspools,
Maybe I should take more crafting schools?

An octopus gives me unsolicited tips,
While I struggle to breathe through the yarny grips.
With every loop, I try to find peace,
But the sweater says, "Try again, at least!"

In this tangled web of joy and doubt,
Who knew crafting could turn me inside out?
I laugh at the chaos, it's perfectly fine,
I'll wear my confusion, it's a new design!

Wandering Between Dreams

In a field of wishes, I skip and prance,
Chasing my thoughts, a curious dance.
The grass whispers secrets, but they're all wrong,
I twirl around, singing a silly song.

Clouds float above, like fluffy advice,
"Take a nap now, or maybe think twice!"
But I'm wide awake, lost in a trance,
With a twinkle in my eye, I take my chance.

The moon winks, says, "Follow your bliss!"
But I bump a tree, oh what did I miss?
A squirrel sighs, "You're a little confused,"
I scratch my head, amused and bemused.

Yet still I wander, laugh at my plight,
In between dreams, I twinkle at night.
As stars play tag across the bright stage,
I'll keep dancing, vibrant and sage!

The Unfinished Journey

I packed my bags, but forgot my shoes,
A map that leads to friendly blues.
The coffee's cold, my thoughts are hot,
Still searching for that magic spot.

My compass spins, and what a tease,
Directions lost among the trees.
With every turn, I trip and fall,
A journey's worth, but where's the call?

A sign that points, yet seems to hide,
Motives wander, nowhere to glide.
I chase the sunset, laugh and sway,
Perhaps tomorrow's a better day.

So here I am, on roads unsure,
Humor my guide, I still endure.
With laughter loud and steps askew,
I'll figure out what to do with you.

Whispers of Tomorrow

I wake each morn, a brand new start,
With toast and dreams, it's quite an art.
The clock ticks fast, then drags its feet,
I juggle hope, not quite complete.

In cafes bright, I sip my brew,
Discussing things that I might do.
With friends who nod, then spill their fries,
We delve in schemes, and half-baked lies.

'Next week, dear pal, I'll write a book!'
But all I draft is how I cook.
The future whispers, a playful ghost,
I chase the toast, I need it most!

Yet humor fills the gaps of doubt,
In silly thoughts, I'm never out.
With each laugh shared, I dare to dream,
Tomorrow's glow, a wobbly beam.

The Inkwell of Ambivalence

With pen in hand, yet ink runs dry,
A canvas bare demands a try.
I sketch a fish that looks like cheese,
A masterpiece? Oh, please, oh please!

I ponder deep, and then I sigh,
A branch of doubt that stretches high.
The choices weigh, not quite the same,
Each path I take—a quirky game.

I dance with hope, yet fall afoul,
My life's a joke, and I'm the owl.
I write the lines of lines unwritten,
As laughter traps the thoughts I'm smitten.

Yet here I stand, with ink-stained hands,
Revising dreams like shifting sands.
In this inkwell, I'll find my way,
Embracing quirks in bright array.

Beyond the Horizon of Dreams

I gaze afar, where skies so blue,
Beyond the hills, what's next to do?
A treasure map drawn in crayon hues,
I follow paths marked by my shoes.

The ocean roars, with waves that laugh,
I'll ride this tide, on a broken raft.
With seagulls squawking wisdom so absurd,
A quirky tale, quite undeterred.

Stars wink at me from realms unknown,
In this grand circus, I'm not alone.
Together we dream, bewildered, blurred,
Chasing those thoughts no one has heard.

So on I journey, through day and night,
With giggles shared, I'll find the light.
Beyond the horizon, with every step,
I'll surf on hopes, no need for prep.

The Road Less Regarded

I wandered down a path quite odd,
With squirrels as my loyal squad.
They chattered loud, gave me a laugh,
I tripped on roots but found my path.

I met a rabbit wearing shoes,
He said, "My friend, you've got the blues!"
I asked him how to clear my head,
He winked and tossed me half a bread.

A breeze rolled in with sweet perfume,
I danced around, dodging the gloom.
Who knew that zany roads could lead,
To all the fun my heart would heed?

So here I stand, a little lost,
Yet laughter bloomed at every cost.
With every step and quirky turn,
I light the flame of joy's sweet burn.

Breadcrumbs in the Wilderness

I left a trail of crumbs so neat,
To find my way, I thought it sweet.
The birds conspired, ate my snack,
Now I'm adrift, no turning back.

I met a fox, he stole my hat,
He grinned and said, "You are quite bat!"
I joined him in a silly dance,
Who knew I'd find my luck by chance?

A deer strutted by in a tutu bright,
Said, "Have some fun, don't dread the night!"
With bouncing steps, we twirled around,
In this lost hood, new friends I found.

So breadcrumbs lost, but laughter found,
In this wild, where joy abounds.
I might not know where I will go,
But silly tales make spirits glow.

Labyrinths of Longing

In a maze of thoughts, I spin and twirl,
With walls so high, oh what a whirl!
Each corner turned, a new surprise,
A llama there with glazed-over eyes.

I asked for wisdom, he just smiled,
"Try a balloon, it's more your style!"
So off I went with floaty cheer,
In this maze, I felt no fear.

I met a cat who loved to sing,
He said, "Just dance, and let joy spring!"
With every twist, I laughed and played,
In baffling paths, my heart was swayed.

So here I stand, still lost in thought,
In swirling fun, I've found the plot.
With giggles bright and spirits high,
A puzzling maze can make you fly.

Crumpled Pages of Expectation

I wrote my dreams in crumpled sheets,
Great plans for my upcoming feats.
They ended up with coffee stains,
But who needs order? My heart reigns!

A paper plane took flight one day,
It swooped and swirled, then flew away.
I chased it down, the world a blur,
"Catch me!" it laughed, "What's the big fur?"

I scribbled notes on napkins bold,
A treasure hunt, my life's pure gold.
Each twist and turn a chance to cheer,
In chaos found, I shifted gears.

So here's to mess and daring schemes,
A life not bound by easy dreams.
In every crumple, laughter sings,
Embrace the chaos that joy brings.

Puzzles Beneath the Surface.

I woke up this morning, where's my shoe?
The cat's got it now, how rude of you!
Coffee spills on the floor, like a new modern art,
Just one more day, let's play it smart.

I search for my keys, please tell me where,
Under the couch? Or maybe the chair?
Life's a riddle with no clear answer in sight,
I'll just wing it, hope it's alright!

The mirror keeps laughing; I join in, too,
A dance with my wrinkles, a well-practiced woo.
Jigsaw pieces under the sofa may hide,
At least the pizza box is my friend in this ride.

In the end, I'll find joy in this game,
Embrace the nonsense, it's all just the same.
Maps of confusion, route's never prepared,
Yet each twist and turn leaves me somewhat ensnared.

Wandering in the Mosaic of Existence.

I'm lost in a world that's a patchwork tile,
Every path I take seems to stretch a mile.
Where does the journey truly begin?
Maybe it's parked where the lost socks have been.

Embracing my chaos like it's a trend,
Finding life lessons in a broken pen.
Imagining life's rules made out of cheese,
Gouda and brie, oh, the ridiculous tease.

A map with no lines, but a few quirky stars,
Reminds me of trips I've taken by car.
Each stop's a surprise, with laughter in tow,
And who needs a plan? Just go with the flow!

So many adventures, confusion, and jest,
In this colorful haze, I'll wear my best vest.
I'll tango with fumbles and prance with delight,
A humor-filled journey, is that not the right?

Threads of Whimsy in the Tapestry.

Once tried to weave a tapestry bright,
But tangled my threads with a laugh and a fright.
I pulled and I yanked, what a curious mess,
Turns out, chaos is my favorite dress!

Each stitch tells a tale of a mishap or two,
Like that time my lunch became a shoe stew.
Who knew spaghetti could fly through the air?
Just a casual Tuesday, no need for despair.

I dance with the looms that make my head spin,
As I boast of my troubles, with a cheeky grin.
Bobbling through life, with yarns all around,
Crafting my story, let giggles abound.

So here's to the knots and the colorful twists,
To finding true freedom where nonsense insists.
Each fray has a story, a laugh, or a tear,
In this whimsical fabric, I've nothing to fear.

In Search of My Northern Star.

Once gazed at the sky, shining bright as a flare,
Thought I saw guidance, but it was just a hare.
Frolicking under moonlight, winking at me,
I pondered my fate, sipping chamomile tea.

Navigating life like it's a board game spree,
With each roll of the dice, I'm just meant to be free.
The compass is spinning, it loves to confuse,
Maybe it's best to just pick and choose.

On a quest for direction, lost in my caper,
I summon my humor like a favorite paper.
With hiccups and giggles, I chase my own tail,
A merry adventure, where laughter won't fail.

With every turn taken, joy's often the guide,
Even if the map drew its own quirky stride.
Aiming for stars with a wink and a grin,
In this raucous expedition, I'm destined to win.

The Ebb and Flow of Aspirations

I dreamed of being a rock star,
But I can't tell a G from C.
So now I'm strumming my own guitar,
In my shower, setting my spirit free.

My life's path seems like a maze,
With signs that are upside down.
Each turn is met with a puzzled gaze,
Wearing my goal like a silly crown.

The universe throws curveballs my way,
And I catch them with a big ol' grin.
I dance like no one's watching today,
The secret? Start with a great spinach bin!

So here's to dreams that shift and sway,
Like jelly on a plate in the sun.
I'll laugh and waltz until I find my way,
Because really, who said it has to be done?

Reflections in a Rippled Pond

I stared at the pond, seeking a sign,
But all I saw were ducks on a spree.
They quacked like philosophers, oh so fine,
"Just float along, mate, and you'll be free!"

My thoughts ripple like stones thrown in haste,
With dreams that bob up and down in a splash.
I tried to catch them, but what a waste,
They do the cha-cha, and I just crash!

A fish swims by, with wisdom so grand,
"Your soul's not a GPS, that's a laugh.
Just make silly plans and take a stand,
Then serve it all up with a side of chaff!"

So here I am, just splashing around,
Ducking under wisdom from the deep.
If life's a circus, where's my clown crown?
I'll join in the dance while the ducks make me weep!

Cracks in the Facade of Certainty

I built a wall, thought it was so grand,
   But then it cracked like an old egg.
  Now wisdom leaks like quicksand,
  And I'm just here wearing a peg-leg.

With plans that flop like a fish on dry land,
  I scribble my notes with a crayon pen.
  I thought I had it all perfectly planned,
But now I'm just chasing my own tail again!

   Certainty is a two-headed beast,
With one head snickering, the other in strife.
  I laugh at my doubts, it's a grand feast,
   And take a selfie with chaos in life.

So here's to the fumbles and silly mistakes,
  Join in my dance, there's fun to be found!
When life gives you lemons, grab some cakes,
And let's make this whole mess quite profound!

Through the Labyrinth of Intentions

I wandered through, a winding maze,
With signs that looked like modern art.
I tripped on thoughts and quirky ways,
My map's a doodle, my compass a tart!

Each turn I take is another surprise,
With twists that make a pretzel proud.
I laugh at the riddles, oh how they rise,
Like popcorn popping, quite loud!

Intentions dance like fireflies at night,
Flitting and flickering here and there.
I chase them down, with all my might,
Only to find out, I just have flair!

So here's to the trip, the bumbles and hops,
With giggles and snorts and all in good cheer.
We'll figure it out when the laughing stops,
Until then, let's just drink cold beer!

Reflections in a Glassy Surface

In the mirror, my hair's in a mess,
What am I doing? I'm feeling the stress.
Thought I was wise, but hey, what a joke,
Chasing the wind with my whims and my smoke.

I tried to be deep, I tried to be grand,
But I tripped on my laces and fell on my hand.
Life's like a puzzle, piece lost in the trash,
Maybe that's wisdom wrapped up in a dash.

My goals are like jelly, they wobble and sway,
Some days I'm genius, on others I stray.
With every sip, I ponder and doubt,
Will I find the answer, or just another route?

So I laugh at my quirks, with each silly twist,
In this grand circus, I simply persist.
Each question I ask leads to more that I find,
But I'm still standing here, with an open mind.

The Intersection of Dreams and Reality

I dreamt I was flying, then fell from the sky,
Reality hit hard; it made me cry.
Chasing some clouds with a pie in my hands,
Turns out they're just thoughts upon shifting sands.

I wore mismatched socks on a Monday so bright,
Intent to make sense, but I'm lost to the night.
Thought I'd write poems that savor and shine,
Instead, I write nonsense and drink cheap red wine.

The more I explore, the less that I know,
Is it me or the world that's putting on a show?
I scribble on napkins, my genius unbound,
But nobody tells me if I'm quite profound.

So I'll dance in the chaos with laughter and glee,
Embrace the absurdity, joyfully free.
At the corner of dreams, may the humor abide,
As I wade through the riddle, quite humorously ride.

Scattered Maps of the Heart

I found a map marked with an 'X' and a grin,
But it led me to nowhere—just old trash and sin.
I followed my heart, or was it my nose?
What's the compass for? Even my coffee just froze.

The road to enlightenment looks like a maze,
With detours and potholes and odd little bays.
Once thought I would travel to find something great,
Now I just wander with snacks on my plate.

I ask all the squirrels, they raise their own tails,
A treasure hunt topsy-turvy with tales.
Can't tell if I'm lost, or I'm simply just here,
With snacks as my guide and my giggles sincere.

Yet in the uproar, I find little leaps,
Laughter's the map that the heart gladly keeps.
So I'll hop through my journey with nibbles and cheer,
In this great treasure hunt, the joy is quite clear.

The Quest for Meaning in Stillness

I sat by the pond, just a moment to think,
Fish swirled around, and I lost my drink.
What's the meaning of silence? I ponder, I stare,
Then a duck quacked loudly—guess it's time to care.

My stillness is loud, it dances and sings,
While I sit with my thoughts, the universe springs.
I hope for an answer in the soft, quiet vibes,
But I'm met with confusion—no wisdom subscribes.

So I flip through my musings like old magazines,
With articles stressing on deep, thoughtful scenes.
But between all the lines, I just find a laugh,
The quest is absurd, like a giraffe in a calf.

I'll take my confusion, with smiles I'll invest,
For the beauty of chaos is honestly best.
In the stillness of questions, my heart will yet shout,
With giggles and whims, I'll just ride it all out.

The Quest for Meaning in the Mundane

In the fridge, a pickle smells like hope,
Dreaming of fame while I fumble the soap.
Laundry piles high, a mountain to climb,
Searching for answers, but losing track of time.

Coffee spills, a paint job on my shirt,
I chase my cat, but she's gone to flirt.
Each cereal box, a puzzle to solve,
Maybe a cracker is where dreams evolve.

Bored with the routine, I try to improvise,
Polishing the TV remote to be wise.
Chasing my tail, I think in a swirl,
But then a dance break makes my head twirl!

So here I stand, a clown in a booth,
Juggling my socks while pursuing the truth.
Laughing at chaos, I'm testing the fate,
A quest that's absurd, but I'm feeling great!

Unraveled Dreams on a Winding Road

Driving in circles, my GPS sighs,
Chasing bright signs, but they're all just lies.
I set off with snacks, thinking I'll roam,
Turns out my heart still wants to go home.

Sunsets like crayons melt in the sky,
I hit a raccoon, should I pause or just cry?
Every twist and turn feels like a silly game,
I'm searching for wisdom, but all I find is fame.

At the rest stop, I ponder, 'Do I need a map?'
While everyone else is taking a nap.
I sip on my coffee, makes me feel wise,
But mostly I'm just good at making bad pies.

When headlights flicker, they dance in my soul,
Winding roads stretch, but I'm still on a roll.
With limbs out the window, wind blowing free,
Unraveled dreams are the best kind of spree!

When the Compass Seems Broken

Woke up one morning, my compass was dead,
North was just south, and I lost all my tread.
I tried to find east, but ended up west,
Navigating life like a poorly-built nest.

Maps are all crumpled, like my sanity too,
Every direction just leads to a zoo.
I ask for some help, a wise man just blinks,
Says, 'Try finding happiness in your kitchen sinks!'

The dog is my co-pilot, he snores through it all,
While I chase down the road like a bouncing ball.
What's true, what's false? Well, that's part of the fun,
When nothing makes sense, then you know you're not done.

With laughter for fuel and puns in the air,
A broken compass leads me knowing I care.
So here I'll wander, with whimsy I'll roam,
Wherever I end up, well, that's still called home!

Dancing with Questions

Twirl to the left, then shimmy to the right,
Questions come knocking in the dead of night.
What's the secret to cheese? To cake? To glee?
I just want to know, why do rhymes come to me?

I ponder my purpose while wearing socks bold,
Underneath the disco lights, my fate's getting sold.
Do I leap like a frog, or glide like a swan?
Maybe just shuffle until the break of dawn.

The answers keep waltzing just out of my sight,
As I juggle my hopes in a comical fight.
With cookies as partners and milk as my muse,
I'll laugh at the riddles, I've nothing to lose.

So bring on the questions, let's dance all around,
Life's curious rhythm is where joy is found.
As the music keeps playing, I'll spin with the flow,
In this dance with confusion, I'm free to just go!

www.ingramcontent.com/pod-product-compliance
Lightning Source LLC
Chambersburg PA
CBHW072139200426
43209CB00051B/158